Festive Foods for the Holidays™

A Christmas Holiday COOKBOOK

Emily Raabe

The Rosen Publishing Group's
PowerKids Press™
New York

The recipes in this cookbook
are intended for a child to make together with an adult.

Many thanks to Ruth Rosen and her test kitchen.

For Rachel, my favorite chef

Published in 2002 by The Rosen Publishing Group, Inc.
29 East 21st Street, New York, NY 10010

First Edition

Book Design: Maria E. Melendez
Project Editor: Frances E. Ruffin

Photo Credits: Cover and title page © Patrick Ramsey MR; pp. 4, 13 © North Wind Pictures; p. 6 © Steve Chenn/CORBIS; p. 7 © Dennis Degnan/CORBIS; p. 8 © Bettmann/CORBIS; pp. 9, 12 © CORBIS; p. 18 © Scott Thode/International Stock; Page number designs illustrated by Maria E. Melendez; All recipe photos by Arlan Dean.

Raabe, Emily.
A Christmas holiday cookbook / Emily Raabe.— 1st ed.
    p. cm. — (Festive foods for the holidays)
Includes index.
  ISBN: 0-8239-5627-X
1. Christmas cookery. 2. Christmas. I. Title. II. Series.
TX739.2.C45 R33 2002
641.5'68—dc21
                                                                00-012979

Manufactured in the United States of America

Contents

The Story of Christmas

On December 25 each year, people of the **Christian** religion celebrate Christmas as the birthday of Jesus Christ. Christians believe that Jesus was the son of God. The story of Christmas tells how Jesus' mother and father, Mary and Joseph, traveled to the town of Bethlehem just before Jesus was born. All of the inns were full in the city of Bethlehem. Mary and Joseph had to take shelter in a **stable**. Jesus was born in the stable among the animals.

Many Christians begin their Christmas celebration on the night of December 24, Christmas Eve. The Christmas season ends on January 6, a day known as the **Epiphany**.

This is a nativity scene with baby Jesus, Mary, and Joseph. Christians in Greece and Eastern Europe celebrate the Epiphany as the most important holiday of the season.

Celebrating Christmas

No one really knows when Jesus was born. **Historians** believe that he lived in the city of Nazareth about 2,000 years ago. In the sixth century, many people in Europe and parts of the Middle East held a midwinter celebration that went from December 17 until January 1. This celebration honored **pagan** gods. People lit candles and bonfires, feasted, and gave gifts. The Christian church wanted people to give up their pagan religion to practice Christianity. The church chose December 25 to celebrate the birth of Jesus, instead of a pagan holiday. Ever since then, December 25 has been celebrated as the birthday of Jesus Christ.

People exchange gifts at Christmas. In the United States, children hang up stockings on Christmas Eve, which are filled with gifts! In Holland, children leave out wooden shoes for gifts.

Saint Nicholas

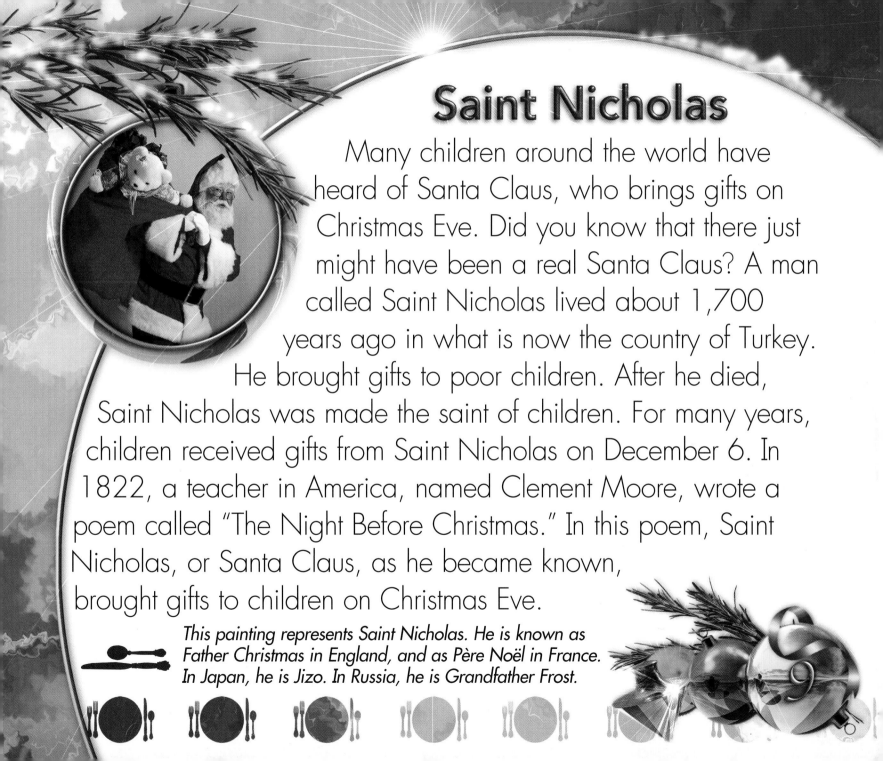

Many children around the world have heard of Santa Claus, who brings gifts on Christmas Eve. Did you know that there just might have been a real Santa Claus? A man called Saint Nicholas lived about 1,700 years ago in what is now the country of Turkey. He brought gifts to poor children. After he died, Saint Nicholas was made the saint of children. For many years, children received gifts from Saint Nicholas on December 6. In 1822, a teacher in America, named Clement Moore, wrote a poem called "The Night Before Christmas." In this poem, Saint Nicholas, or Santa Claus, as he became known, brought gifts to children on Christmas Eve.

This painting represents Saint Nicholas. He is known as Father Christmas in England, and as Père Noël in France. In Japan, he is Jizo. In Russia, he is Grandfather Frost.

Christmas Sweets

Christmas is a time for eating delicious food, especially sweets. In England, people eat plum pudding after their Christmas dinner. In Norway, the Christmas Eve dinner might include seven different kinds of cookies! Norwegian children make paper baskets that they hang on their Christmas trees. They fill these baskets with candies and nuts. In Eastern Europe, Christmas cookies often are made with nuts, raisins, flour, cinnamon, and sugar. Italian children eat a kind of sugar paste, called nougat, filled with nuts and dried fruits at Christmastime.

Christmas cookies also can be butter or chocolate cookies, which are cut in Christmas shapes. Gingerbread people are wonderful Christmas cookies. Cutout cookies are easy to make and fun to decorate.

2 1833 04331 7343

Christmas Gingerbread People

⅔ cup (160 l)
dark
molasses
½ cup (118 ml)
butter
icing in a tube

You will need:

2 ¾ cups (651ml) flour
3 teaspoons (15 ml)
   baking soda
1 teaspoon (5 ml) each
   of ground cloves,
   ginger, cinnamon
½ teaspoon (2.5 ml)
   salt
¼ (1.2 ml) teaspoon
   allspice
1 beaten egg
1 cup (327 ml) brown
   sugar

How to do it:

Preheat oven to 375 ° Fahrenheit (191 °C).

Sift the dry ingredients into a large bowl.
   Combine the egg, brown sugar, molasses,
   and butter in another bowl. Mix well.

Stir the liquid mixture into the dry mixture. Mix
   the dough until all the flour is blended in.
   Divide the dough in half and roll out on a
   floured board. The rolled dough should be
   about ⅓ inch (.8 m) thick.

Cut out your cookies with a floured cookie cutter.

Use nuts, raisins, or seeds for buttons, eyes,
   noses, and mouths. Bake until lightly
   browned – about 12 minutes.

Let cookies cool. Decorate with
   white icing from a tube.

Christmas Decorations

At Christmas, people decorate their homes and churches with lights, evergreen branches, and red, green, gold, and silver decorations. In Europe and North America, many families also have Christmas trees in their homes. Ornaments made from paper, glass, silver, and gold brighten the trees. Mistletoe has been used to decorate homes during Christmas for thousands of years. Until recent times, the church would not let people hang mistletoe because it had been used in pagan **rituals**. The church replaced mistletoe with holly, another plant with pointed leaves and red berries. Today people decorate with both holly and mistletoe.

Many years ago, people lit their Christmas trees with candles. This was beautiful but dangerous. The trees sometimes caught on fire. Today people use electric lights to decorate their trees.

Christmas Eve

Christmas Eve is an important part of the Christmas celebration. Many people go to church for midnight **Mass** on Christmas Eve. During the midnight Mass, people light candles and sing **carols**. This is how they welcome the baby Jesus into the world, as Christmas Eve turns into Christmas morning.

In many countries of the world, Christmas Eve is more important than Christmas Day. In Poland, Christmas Eve is said to be a magical time. Polish **legend** has it that animals can speak on Christmas Eve. In the United States, American children often leave out a snack for Santa to eat when he stops by their houses to deliver presents. You could leave Santa some gingerbread cookies, and perhaps a nice, warm mug of mulled cider to drink with his cookies!

Mulled Cranberry Cider

How to do it:

Pour the cider into a medium-size pot.

Chop the cranberries coarsely with a knife.

Add the cranberries and all of the other ingredients to the cider. Have an adult help to heat the mixture until it is almost boiling.

Turn the heat down and simmer for 20 minutes.

Pour the liquid through a strainer into a serving container, discarding the spices and cranberries. Serve hot or cold.

This recipe serves four people.

For Santa

You will need:

1 quart (946 ml) of apple cider

1 cup (237 ml) fresh cranberries

¼ tsp (1.3 ml) cardamom

3 whole cloves

1 cinnamon stick

¼ cup (59 ml) of honey

Christmas Feasts

Christmas is a time for families and friends to gather for a feast to celebrate the holiday season. Some Italian Christians **fast** all day on Christmas Eve. Then they sit down at night to a huge feast of eels and a special spaghetti dish. In southern Italy, families eat seven kinds of fish or seafood. The fish is a **symbol** of Christ. In Russia, the Christmas feast might include beet soup and stuffed cabbage. In England and the United States, many people eat roast turkey, goose, roast beef, or other meats for their meal. You could make Cornish game hens for your feast. Cornish game hens are popular in the United States and in England, especially at Christmastime.

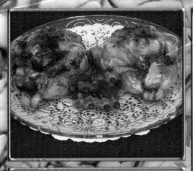

You will need:

4 Cornish game hens (You can get these at a supermarket, or from a butcher.)
2 lemons, cut in half
salt, pepper, and garlic powder
parsley
One jar of cranberry jelly or relish
butter or olive oil

How to do it:

If the game hens are frozen, defrost them. Have an adult help to rinse them well in cool water. Remove any giblets from inside the hens.

Preheat oven to 375 ° Fahrenheit (191 °C).

Sprinkle hens with salt, pepper, and garlic powder, inside and out. Rub spices into the hens' skin.

Rub each bird with a lemon half. Slice the lemon in half and place it inside each bird, with the parsley.

Roast the Cornish game hens in the oven for 45–60 minutes, depending on the size of the hens (Have an adult help you decide when the hens are done.)

About 30 minutes into roasting, have an adult help to spoon the cranberry jelly or relish over the birds.

Serves 4 people.

Christmas Traditions

Christmas has many **traditions**, from singing carols to giving gifts to lighting candles at night. In America, people often go from house to house singing Christmas carols on Christmas Eve. Children in Puerto Rico and in Spain put their shoes under the Christmas tree on the night of Epiphany, or Three Kings Night. In the morning, their shoes are full of gifts from the three kings. In Mexico and in the southwestern part of the United States, the Christmas celebration begins on December 16. On that night, called Posada, people parade through the town to remember how Joseph and Mary searched for a place to sleep on the night that Jesus was born.

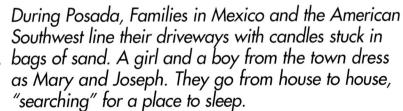

During Posada, Families in Mexico and the American Southwest line their driveways with candles stuck in bags of sand. A girl and a boy from the town dress as Mary and Joseph. They go from house to house, "searching" for a place to sleep.

Christmas Food in America

The early settlers in America came from England, Germany, Holland, France, Spain, and other countries. They all had different ways of celebrating Christmas and different foods that they liked to eat. People in the United States enjoy food that comes from many different traditions. People in the southern part of the United States might eat collard greens, sweet potatoes, and ham for Christmas. In New England, a Christmas meal might be roast beef and Yorkshire pudding, or a Christmas ham. Rainbow Jell-O salad is an example of an all-American dish that you could make for your family and friends.

Rainbow Salad

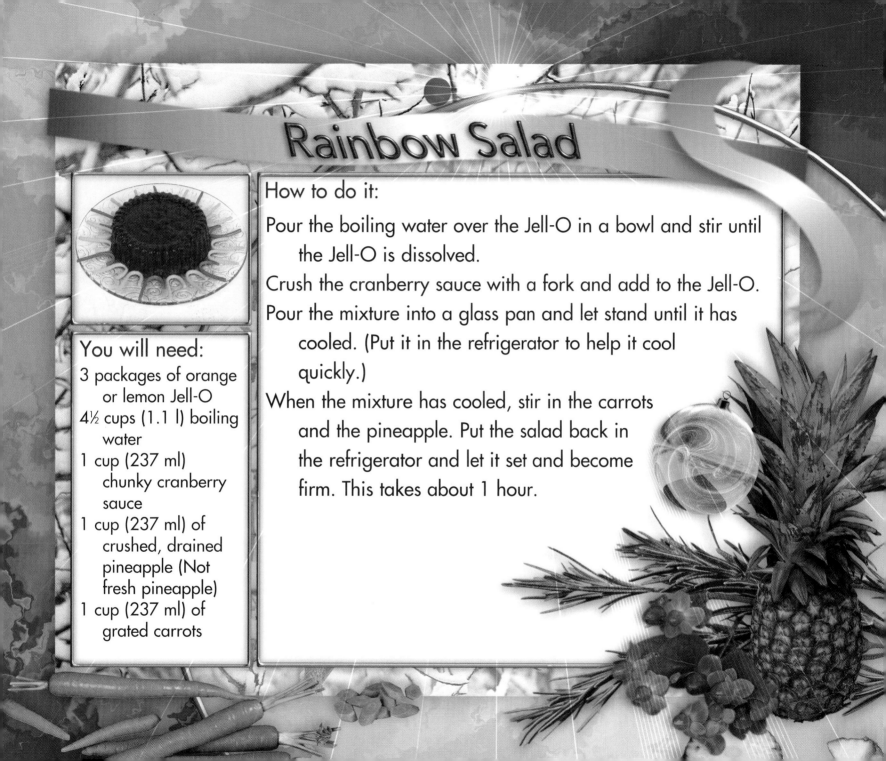

You will need:

3 packages of orange or lemon Jell-O

4½ cups (1.1 l) boiling water

1 cup (237 ml) chunky cranberry sauce

1 cup (237 ml) of crushed, drained pineapple (Not fresh pineapple)

1 cup (237 ml) of grated carrots

How to do it:

Pour the boiling water over the Jell-O in a bowl and stir until the Jell-O is dissolved.

Crush the cranberry sauce with a fork and add to the Jell-O.

Pour the mixture into a glass pan and let stand until it has cooled. (Put it in the refrigerator to help it cool quickly.)

When the mixture has cooled, stir in the carrots and the pineapple. Put the salad back in the refrigerator and let it set and become firm. This takes about 1 hour.

Christmas Around the World

Christmas is celebrated by people in many countries in the world. In France, people go to church on Christmas Eve, then have a feast at midnight. They might eat oysters, ham, pastries, and drink wine. People in Finland put candles on the graves of their loved ones on Christmas Eve. In Poland, families eat a 12-course meal on Christmas Eve. The 12 courses **represent** Jesus' closest followers, who were known as the 12 **disciples**. In New York City, a grand parade on Thanksgiving begins the Christmas season. People in the United States celebrate until New Year's Day. Wherever Christmas is celebrated, it is always one of the most joyful holidays in the Christian religion.

Glossary

carols (KAR-ulz) Songs, usually sung in groups at Christmas.

Christian (KRIS-chun) Someone who follows the teachings of Jesus Christ and the Bible.

disciples (dih-SY-pulz) Followers of Jesus Christ in his lifetime.

Epiphany (eh-PIH-fuh-nee) The name for the day when the three wise men, or kings, visited the baby Jesus.

fast (FAST) To go without food.

historians (hih-STOR-ee-unz) People who study history.

legend (LEH-jend) A story that is passed down through time that many people believe to be true.

Mass (MAS) A church service in the Catholic church.

pagan (PAY-gen) A religion that is not Jewish, Christian, or Muslim. Pagan religions often worship many gods and goddesses.

represent (reh-prih-ZENT) To stand for.

rituals (RIH-choo-ulz) Religious ceremonies.

stable (STAY-bul) A building that shelters horses, cattle, and other animals.

symbol (SIM-bul) An object or design that stands for something important.

traditions (truh-DIH-shunz) Way of doing something that are passed down through the years.

Index

Web Sites

To learn more about Christmas, check out this Web site:
www.christmas.com/worldview